TRAILER PARK
PARQUE DE REMOLQUES

Written by J.C. Dillard

Illustrations by Anna Usacheva

Translation by Madelin Arroyo Romero

HARDBALL PRESS

Trailer Park\ Parque De Remolques
Copyright © 2017 by J.C. DIllard
This book is a work of fiction. Names, characters, places and incidents are either the product of the author's imagination, or, if real, used fictitiously.
No part of this book may be reproduced or transmitted in any form or by an electronic or mechanical means, including photocopying, recording or by any information storage and retrieval system, without the express written permission of the publisher, except where permitted by law.
Published by Hard Ball Press.
Information available at: www.hardballpress.com
ISBN: 978-0-9991358-3-9
Story by J.C. DIllard
Illustrations by Anna Usacheva
Translated by Madelin Arroyo Romero
Cover art by Anna Usachev
Cover & interior design by D. Bass

DEDICATION

For My Family

Robert's family moved to the trailer park last Saturday.

"Here's our new neighborhood," said Robert's dad.

"This isn't a real neighborhood," said Robert. "This is a trailer park."

La familia de Humberto se mudó al parque de remolques el sábado pasado.

"Aquí está nuestro nuevo vecindario," dijo el papá de Humberto.

"Este no es un vecindario real," dijo Humberto. "Este es un parque de remolques."

On Sunday, Robert sat on his front step. Ever since his dad lost his job, everything had changed, and Robert didn't like it.

El domingo, Humberto se sentó en sus escaleras de enfrente. Desde que su papá perdió su trabajo, todo había cambiado.

The girl next door waved. "I'm Jessie. Want to play?"
"No," said Robert. "I want to play with my real friends
--at my real home."
"Isn't this your home?" asked Jessie.

La niña de a lado saludó. "Soy Sofía. ¿Quieres jugar?"
"No," dijo Humberto. "Yo quiero jugar con mis amigos
verdaderos—en mi casa verdadera."
"¿No es ésta tu casa?" preguntó Sofía.

Robert pulled a road map from his pocket and pointed.

"That's where my home is. It has an upstairs, a big back yard, and my swing set." He stuffed the map back in his pocket. "I want to go home."

Humberto sacó un mapa vial de su bolsillo y apuntó.

"Ahí está mi casa. Tiene un segundo piso, un patio trasero grande, y mi columpio." Metió su mapa de nuevo en su bolsillo. "Quiero regresar a casa."

On Monday morning, Robert found a new map taped to his door.

El lunes en la mañana, Humberto encontró un mapa nuevo pegado en su puerta.

Robert followed the map. Jessie was swinging on a tire in Mr. Watson's oak tree.
"Hi, jungle explorer," said Jessie. "Seen any tigers lately?"
"This isn't a jungle," said Robert. "This is a trailer park."
Jessie nodded. "Then would you like a turn on the swing?"
"No!" Robert turned and ran away.

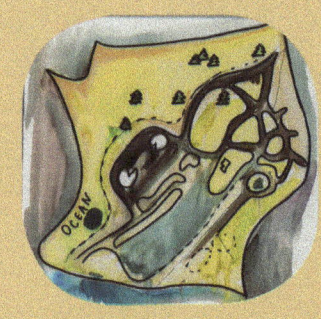

Humberto siguió el mapa. Sofía se columpiaba en una llanta en el árbol de roble del Sr. Arroyo.
"Hola, explorador de la selva," dijo Sofía. "¿Haz visto algún tigre últimamente?"
"Esto no es una selva," dijo Humberto. "Esto es un parque de remolques."
Sofía asintió con la cabeza. "¿Entonces te gustaría un turno en el columpio?"
"¡No!" Humberto se dió la vuelta y corrió.

On Tuesday morning, Robert found another map on his door.
Robert followed the map. Jessie was crouched in a weedy ditch, chasing tadpoles with Ahmed and Amelia.

OCEAN

El martes en la mañana, Humberto encontró otro mapa en su puerta.
Humberto siguió el mapa. Sofía estaba agachada en una zanja, persiguiendo renacuajos con Valeria y Erika.

He walked down the gravel path—and stopped.

Él caminó por la calle de grava—y se detuvo.

"But I do like catching tadpoles."
Jessie sailed across the ocean with the brave crew, chasing a great whale.
Robert waded in the water and caught three tadpoles.

Pero sí me gusta atrapar renacuajos."
Sofía trasnavegó el océano con la tripulación valiente, persiguiendo a una gran ballena.
Humberto chapoteó en el agua y atrapó tres renacuajos.

On Wednesday morning, Robert found another map on his door.

El miércoles en la mañana, Humberto encontró otro mapa en su puerta.

Robert followed the map. Jessie was balancing across Mrs. Garcia's clothesline.
"Hello, lion tamer," said Jessie. "Are you ready to perform tricks with two ferocious beasts?"
Robert shook his head. "What beasts?"
Jessie pointed at Mrs. Garcia's two dogs, Jefe and Pepe.
Robert laughed.

Humberto siguió el mapa. Sofía estaba parada enfrente de los perros sosteniendo una vara como si fuera un director de circo.
"Hola, domador de leones," dijo Sofía. "¿Estás listo para realizar trucos con dos bestias feroces?"
Humberto movió la cabeza. "¿Cuales bestias?"
Sofía apuntó a los perros de la Sra. Martínez, Jefe y Pepe.
Humberto se rió.

Jessie walked the tightrope, and Robert tamed the lions.
Mrs. Garcia looked out her window and clapped. "¡Magnífico!"

Sofía caminó por cuerda floja y Humberto domó a los leones.
La Sra. Martínez miró por su ventana y aplaudió. "¡Magnífico"

On Thursday morning, Robert found another map on his door.

El jueves en la mañana, Humberto encontró otro mapa en su puerta.

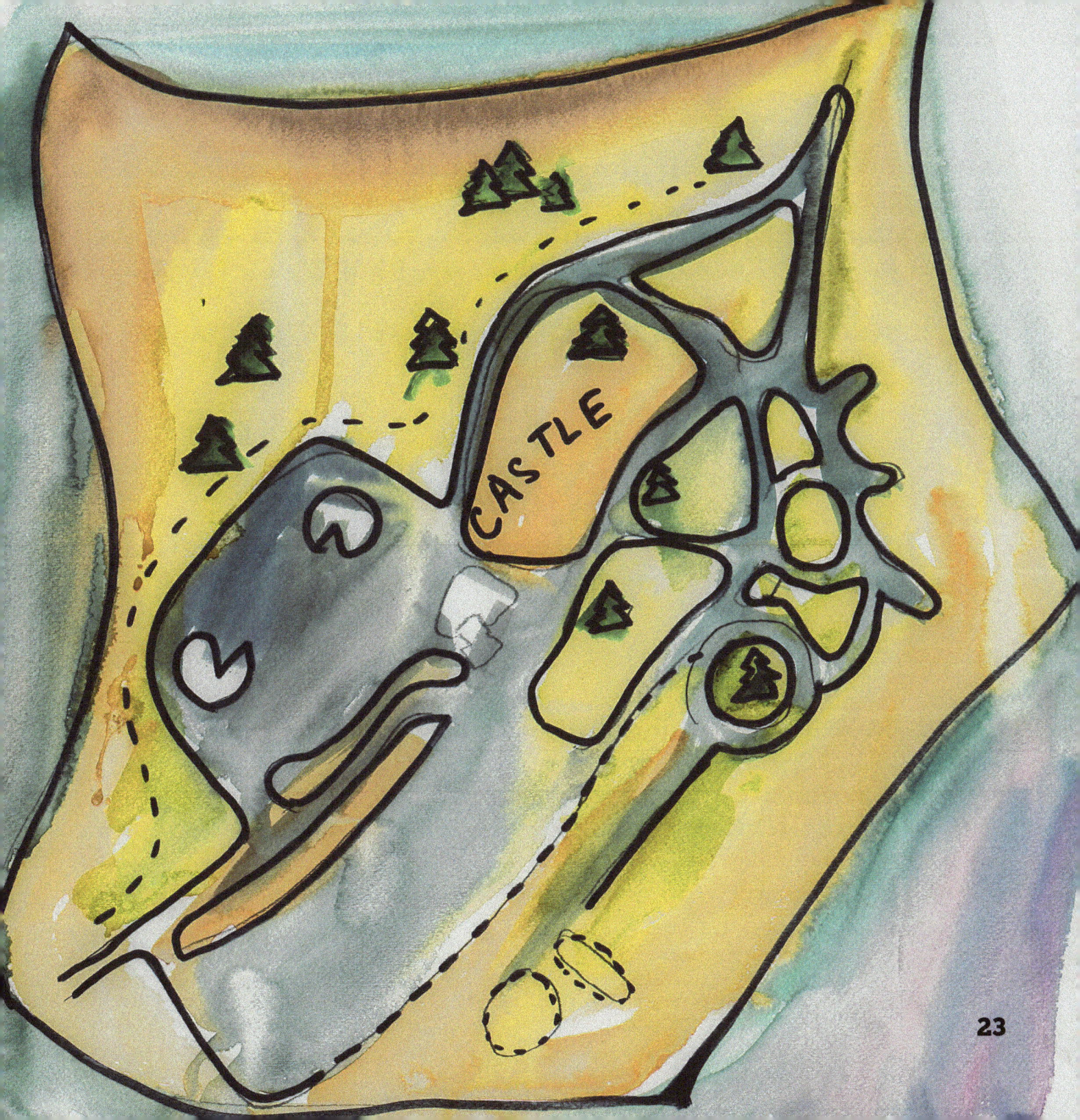

Robert followed the map. Jessie was eating strawberries in Miss Kim's garden.
"Good day, Sir Robert," said Jessie.
Robert bowed. "Good day, Queen Jessie. Shall I slay this wicked dragon?"
"No, indeed," said Jessie. "She is a good dragon, ridding the land of thieves."

Humberto siguió el mapa. Sofía estaba comiendo fresas en el jardín de la Srta. María.
"Buen día, don Humberto," dijo Sofía.
Humberto se inclinó, "Buen día, reina Sofía. ¿Mató al dragón malvado?"
"No, de hecho, no," dijo Sofía. "Ella es una buena dragona, librándo la tierra de los ladrones."

While the dragon roamed the countryside,
Sir Robert and Queen Jessie ate a medieval feast.

Mientras el dragón recorría el campo,
don Humberto y la reina Sofía comieron en un banquete medieval.

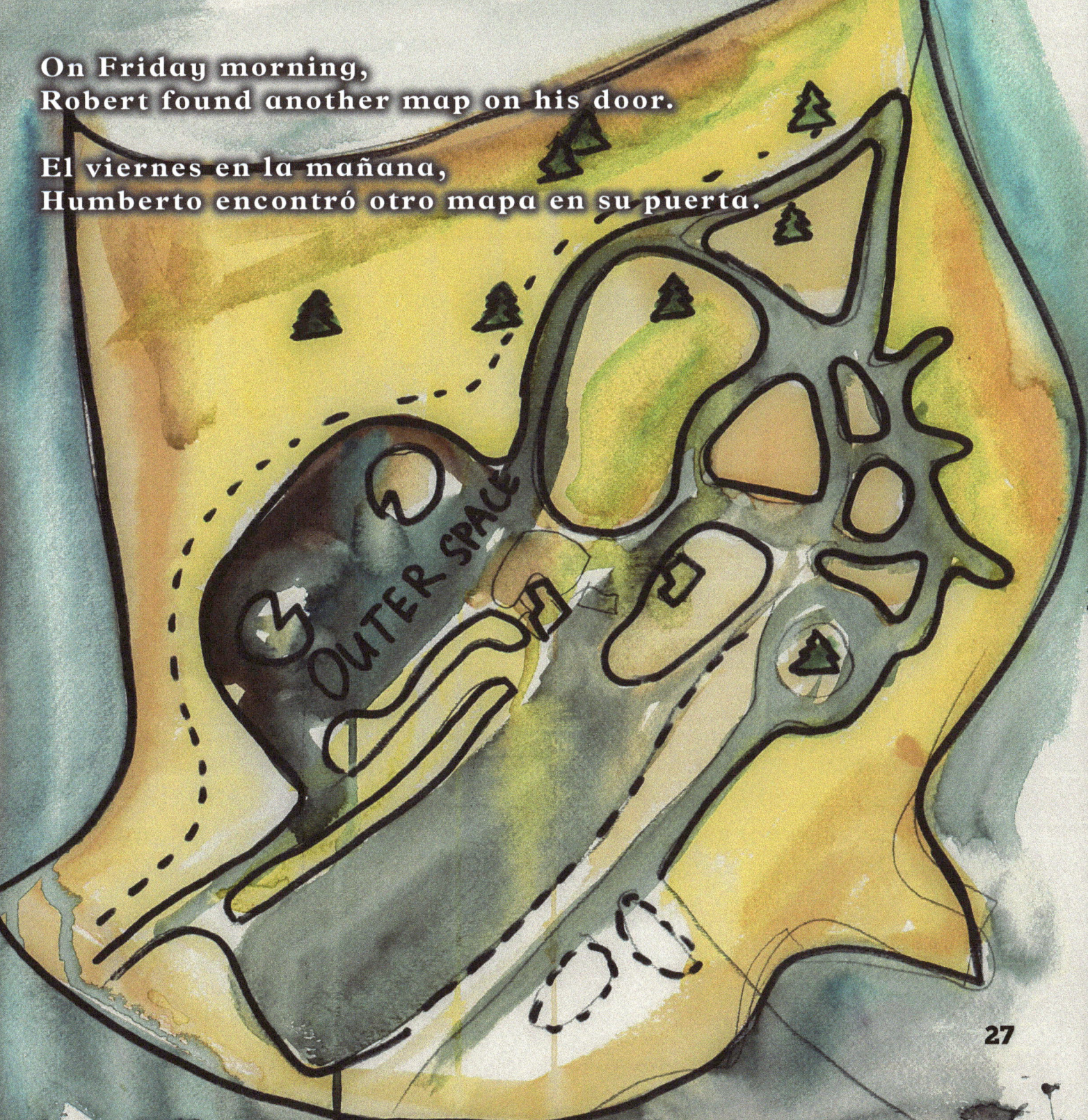

On Friday morning,
Robert found another map on his door.

El viernes en la mañana,
Humberto encontró otro mapa en su puerta.

Robert followed the map. Jessie and José were playing in the back of Mr. Lopez's truck.
"Mission control to space station," Robert said. "Countdown in five...four...three...two...one!"
He leaped into the truck. "Blast off!" they shouted.

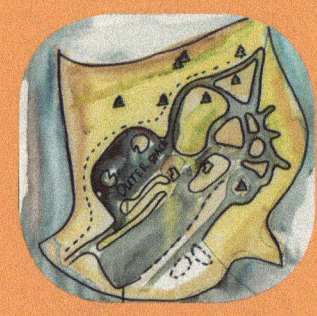

Humberto siguió el mapa. Sofía y José estaban jugando en la parte trasera de la camioneta del Sr. Cervantes.
"Torre de control llamando a la estación espacial," Humberto dijo. "¡Cuenta regresiva en cinco...cuatro... tres... dos... uno!"
Saltó en la camioneta. "¡Despegue!" los dos gritaron.

Three astronauts soared through space, dodging meteors and catching stardust.
Tres astronautas volaron por el espacio, esquivando meteoritos y atrapando polvo estelar.

On Saturday, Jessie found a map on *her* door.

El sábado, Sofía encontró un mapa en *su* puerta.

So did Mr. Watson, Ahmed and Amelia, Mrs. Garcia, Miss Kim, José, Mr. Lopez, and all the other neighbors in the trailer park. They followed the maps and found music and balloons.

Y también el Sr. Arroyo, Valeria y Erika, la Sra. Martínez , la Srta. María, José , el Sr. Cervantes y todos los otros vecinos del parque de remolques.
Ellos siguieron el mapa y encontraron música y globos.

They found a cake, a grill, and three pitchers of lemonade.
And they found Robert with a big smile on his face.

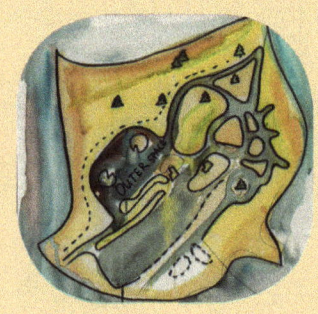

Encontraron un pastel, un asador, y tres jarras de limonada.
Y encontraron a Humberto con una gran sonrisa en su cara.

"Is this a county fair?" asked Jessie. "A gnome's birthday? Or a coronation for a king?"
"Even better," said Robert. "It's a surprise party—for my new friends in my new neighborhood!"

"¿Esta es una feria del condado?" pregunto Sofía. "¿Un cumpleaños de gnomo? ¿O una coronación para un rey?"
"Aún mejor," dijo Humberto. "!Es una fiesta sorpresa—para mis nuevos amigos en mi nueva vecindad!"

QUESTONS FOR TEACHERS, LIBRARIANS AND PARENTS TO ASK CHILDREN

1. Moving to a new neighborhood can be scary. You might miss your old room, your old house, and your old friends. If a new boy or girl moved into your neighborhood, what could you do to help them feel at home?

2. Robert moved from a big home in a fancy neighborhood to a trailer park. He gave up his swing set and his own room and his own backyard. But in his new neighborhood he found fun places to play in and explore. How do you think the trailer park compared to his old home for fun things to do and see?

3. We don't know who Robert's neighbors were when he lived in his old house. But we do know that his new neighbors in the trailer park, like Ahmed and Amelia, Mrs. Garcia and Miss Kim, are from different countries and different cultures. How can having diverse neighbors make a neighborhood an even better place to live?

4. Making new friends can be difficult. When you meet new people, you may be afraid they won't like you. What did Jessie do to show Robert that his new neighbors were happy to welcome him?

5. Robert's new friend Jessie has a big imagination. She pretends that a little creek is an ocean, that Mrs. Garcia's dogs are circus lions, that chickens are dragons, and that Mr. Lopez's truck is a space station. What do you like to pretend when you play with your friends?

PREGUNTAS PARA MAESTROS, BIBLIOTECARIOS Y PADRES PARA HACERLE A LOSNIÑOS

1. Moverse a una vecindad nueva puede ser aterrador. Puede que extrañes tu antiguo cuarto, tu antigua casa, o tus antiguos amigos. ¿Si una niña o niño nuevo se moviera a tu vecindad, que puedes hacer tú para ayudarle a sentirse en casa?

2. Humberto se mudo de una casa grande en una vecindad bonita a un parque de remolques. Él perdió su columpio y su propio cuarto y su propio patio. Pero en su nueva vecindad él encontró lugares divertidos para jugar y explorar. ¿Como piensas tú que se compara el parque de remolques con su antigua casa de cosas divertidas que hacer y ver?

3. No sabemos quienes eran los vecinos de Humberto cuando vivía en su antigua casa. Pero si sabemos que sus nuevos vecinos en el parque de remolques como, Valeria y Erika, la Sra. Martínez y la Srta. María, son de diferentes países y de diferentes culturas. ¿Como el tener vecinos diversos puede hacer una vecindad un lugar aún mejor para vivir?

4. Hacer nuevos amigos puede ser difícil. Cuando tú conoces a gente nueva, te puede dar temor a que no les caigas bien. ¿Que hizo Sofía para enseñarle a Humberto que sus nuevos vecinos estaban felices de darle la bienvenida?

5. La nueva amiga de Humberto, Sofía tiene una gran imaginación. Ella pretende que un arroyo es un océano, que los perros de la Sra. Martínez son leones de circo, que las gallinas son dragones, y que la camioneta del Sr. Cervantes es una nave espacial. ¿A ti que te gusta pretender cuando juegas con tus amigos?

ABOUT THE AUTHOR, ILLUSTRATOR AND TRANSLATOR

J.C. Dillard has several young children who keep her on her toes, an attorney husband who fights the good fight for Mississippi workers, and a storage unit full of books that won't fit in their house.

Anna Usacheva is a young artist from Samara, Russia. In Samara she studied art at the Waldorf Middle School. A recent immigrant to the United States, she continues to study art and to develop her English language skills at the City University of New York.

Madelin is a first generation college student who completed her BA in Spanish and minor in Math & Science Education at UCSB in 2012. Born in Mexico City and raised in Los Angeles, she fought hard for the Dream Act as an AB540 student during her undergrad. She has been teaching and traveling ever since and currently works as an ESL Instructor at a local city college working with the community.

CHILDREN'S BOOKS from HARD BALL PRESS

Joelito's Big Decision, La gran Decisión de Joelito:
Ann Berlak (Author), Daniel Camacho (Illustrator),
José Antonio Galloso (Translator)

Manny and the Mango Tree, Many y el Árbol de Mango:
Alí R. and Valerie Bustamante (Authors), Monica Lunot-Kuker (Illustrator). Mauricio Niebla (Translator)

The Cabbage That Came Back, El Repollo que Volvió
Stephen Pearl & Rafael Pearl (Authors), Rafael Pearl (Illustrator), Sara Pearl (Translator)

Hats Off For Gabbie, ¡Aplausos para Gaby!:
Marivir Montebon (Author), Yana Murashko (Illustrator), Mauricio Niebla (Translator)

Margarito's Forest/El Bosque de Don Margarito:
Andy Carter (Author), Alison Havens (Illustrator), Sergio Villatoro (Graphic Design),
Artwork contributions by the children of the Saq Ja' elementary school
K'iche tranlations by Eduardo Elas and Manuel Hernandez
Translated by Omar Mejia

Jimmy's Carwash Adventure, La Aventura de Jaime en el Autolavado:
Victor Narro (Author), Yana Murashko (Illustrator), Madelin Arroyo (Translator)

Good Guy Jake/Buen Chico Jake,
Mark Torres (author), Yana Murashko (illustrator), Madelin Arroyo (translator)

Polar Bear Pete's Ice Is Melting!
Timothy Sheard (author), Kayla Fils-Amie (illustrator), Madelin Arroyo (translator)

HOW TO ORDER BOOKS:

Order books from www.hardballpress.com, Amazon.com, or independent booksellers everywhere.

Receive a 20% discount for orders of 10 or more, a 40% discount for orders of 50 or more when ordering from www.hardballpress.com.

www.ingramcontent.com/pod-product-compliance
Lightning Source LLC
Chambersburg PA
CBHW061147010526
44118CB00026B/2896